MW01138717

A Simple Truth

A SIMPLE TRUTH

Find Your Destiny

Using the 20-Day Symbols of the Aztec Calendar

LUIS ARMANDO RODRIGUEZ CEDILLO

AND

CHARLES DAVID HAGEN

Red Bear Press and Xochitl Publishing
"A SIMPLE TRUTH"

Find Your Destiny
Using the 20-Day Symbols of the Aztec Calendar

Written by
Charles David Hagen and
Luis Rodriguez Armando Cedillo

Illustrations from
Codex Borgia and Codex Borbonico

Designed by
BIRDWALK STUDIO
Blue Hill, ME

All rights are reserved. This book may not be reproduced or transmitted in any form or by any means, electronic, mechanical, including photocopying, recording or by any information storage and retrieval systems, without written permission from the authors, except by a reviewer, who may quote brief passages in a review.

A Simple Truth © 2011
First Edition
www.asimpletruth.org
asimpletruth20@gmail.com

ISBN: 978-0-9896153-6-5

Second Edition 2013
by
Red Bear Press
192 Main Street
Ellsworth, Maine 04605
redbearpublishing.com

This book is dedicated to the Ancestors,
to the Elders, and the Children—
now and in the future.

We would like to gratefully acknowledge
the editing help of John Nagy and for
believing that this flower
could blossom.

Contents

"At Last My Heart Knows It"

At last my heart knows it
At last my heart knows it
I hear a song
I contemplate a flower
May they never fade

"I Remember What I Left Behind"

What will I leave with?
Nothing left of me in the earth.
How is my heart to react?
Did we come here in vain to live above the land?
At least we left flowers.
At least we left songs.

These are portions of two poems written by Netzahualcoyotl
a poet, leader and man of divine wisdom.

(I Rabbit. 1402-6 Flint, 1472)
who was from Tezcoco, Mexico

Aztec Calendar

Prologue

Before you start your journey it is important to get some background on how "A Simple Truth" came about. The words you are going to read did not come from some revelation Luis or I had. This knowledge about the existence of humans was created by great minds many centuries ago. "A Simple Truth" shares this message that has survived. The ideas and concepts came from the Toltec people who studied and had an understanding of themselves, this planet, universe and everything around them.

Allow me to share some background about events that helped to create this book. Around 1990 a group of us from the North (New England mostly) went to Mexico at the invitation of Tlakaelel, a Mexica Elder, who was speaking of 1992 being the year to demonstrate the survival of Indigenous culture, instead of it being the year to celebrate the 500th Anniversary of Columbus discovering America.

When we arrived in Mexico we were overwhelmed with the language barriers and unfamiliar customs. Then we met Luis, ever the teacher, who shared what was expected of us and how we should carry ourselves. He showed us by example, with patience, but also expecting us to really understand their traditions. We didn't just learn how to do the movements in these events but 'why' we did them that way. The 'why' of these things drew me in and Luis began to share thoughts and ideas with me.

Luis and I talked about many things. We traveled together to many places, ceremonies and events over the past two decades. He gave me titles of books for me to get a more in-depth understanding of what he was teaching me. I began learning things that were only shared or explained with few people outside of the Toltec culture, for more than the past five hundred years.

In the summer of 2008 Luis and I were driving to my family home in Maine. We began talking again about the 20 day symbols on the Aztec calendar, their meaning and the importance of the order of the symbols. I finally felt that the 20 day symbols were connected to the human experience and they all had a place in each of us. I even began to understand why Xochitl the flower is the 20th symbol — the most beautiful thing we see.

Luis was excited and said, "Yes! I think you are getting it but remember this is only the beginning." Now Luis and I are sharing this message with everyone. We hope you understand the connection of each symbol as they go from one to twenty, for they are part of us and a part of us every day. This statement is important to remember.

This is my story of receiving knowledge but now it becomes your story about receiving knowledge and what you do with it.

We are all part of the story, we are all flowers.

~ C.D.H.

Foreword

Where did these ideas come from?
by Luis Armando Rodriguez Cedillo

Charles (Chuck) Hagen is a good friend of mine. In the last twenty years we have shared ceremonies, teachings and conversations, both of us continuing to learn together throughout this time.

Our connection comes from Chuck's attention to and understanding of pre-Hispanic Mexico. He is considered "Mexika." I use this word to speak of someone who participates and is involved with the culture of my country, Mexico.

Chuck had the vision to create this book to be able to reach people in a simple way, but also to make this message appeal to everyone who is trying to improve their life.

We both share a desire to do this with respect and consideration for all of the ancestors who gave their lives to make it possible for this knowledge to survive.

Chuck was touched by the spirit and was moved by this huge emotion to know and understand the value of this culture, the same culture that others have denied existed and believed to be forgotten by some of the descendants of Mexico itself.

The intention has always been to share this culture with a sensitivity and emotion for this great treasure, which is the knowledge. This knowledge everyone can use without distinction to their color, sex, religion, or any other excuse. We all are the expression of the Creator, and we are all human beings.

We must behave like sisters and brothers because we are Creator. I am really thankful to this foreigner that he was touched by this knowledge, love and respect for this path.

About the Authors

The creation of this book was inspired by the elders and those who went before us—it is for them. It says we remember them.

Luis and Chuck have shared time and thoughts together, and this book comes from those thoughts and concepts, along with Luis's willingness to work with Chuck; but also the elders allowing these concepts to be shared by everyone.

Chuck has studied the culture that was Mexico before the invasion of the Spanish, but will say he is just beginning and does not want anyone to think he is claiming to be an expert on this culture. He is indebted to Luis and all the others for sharing this knowledge with him.

This book is about sharing that universal message left for us, the human beings by the ancestors and now shared through these pages. Here is some background on this special human being, Luis.

Luis Armando Rodríguez Cedillo is a true Mexican or Mexika. Since he was a small boy he has been taught the pre-Hispanic culture of Mexico having many elders share their knowledge of the ancestors with him throughout his life's journey. He is a philosopher, a professor, a bee keeper, and has knowledge of astronomy, mathematics, and many other attributes. He has spent his life studying the culture that was pre-Hispanic Mexico. He views the universe with an all encompassing view, able to look at things scientifically and mathematically, yet also share the philosophical point of view in a way even a person just meeting him would understand.

He is sharing the key that will open the door to a different way of viewing the universe. The key will open the door to us all finding our purpose and destiny. We are going to connect the dots of the messages carved in stone thousands of years ago presenting a view that we will own. We will have our truth or Tonalli. What we do with it, and how we do it will be our own journey.

This book can show us the things needed to live our lives in balance, and how to maintain balance. Whether we are doctors, lawyers, construction workers, athletes, parents, students or children. It can help anyone who can read or hear it from someone else. In these pages you will find a unique message shared by Luis and Chuck.

An Invitation

Dear Reader:

This is an unfinished book and does not have a beginning or end. It is the same for all that exists. The basis of it is lost in the region of time and space.

At the start of Creation comes the interrelationship between everything. This interrelationship makes possible the universe, our solar system, our Mother Earth, all life and ourselves—the human beings.

This invitation is to join in this adventure that is our life and the light itself. Most of us believe our existence begins with our birth and ends with our death. Is this the way it really is?

If we can open our minds and think about our mothers and fathers still living in us, we can also think that everything that has come before us is also living in us, and not just as humans, it is the same for all that exists, we are all the culmination of everything. The things we eat and breathe and also the material we are made from, have the same age as the whole universe.

This means we all have the same age in terms of existence as the Universe. We are the synthesis of Creation. We are a link in this huge chain that we called existence, but at the same time we have a commitment to the coming generations with all things, not just humans.

What is that commitment? Maybe we do not realize it, but we are impulsed to accomplish and be part of this project we know as Creation.

The creation of us is the sign of the existence of our species, but not just humans; it is the same for the animals, plants, stars, everything in the universe. We are able to create. We are what we create and we start to ask ourselves, "Who are we?" "Where do we come from and why are we here?"

What is our purpose? Sometimes the answer comes before we have the question, but sometimes the answer is not so clear. The majority of us ignore who we are and what we are supposed to be; sometimes this causes us to not achieve the meaning and commitment of our lives. Our destiny is an understanding of the knowledge of ourselves. This is the reason we have been created. We call this our "Tonalli" (destiny).

This is an invitation for all of us to find happiness by understanding the knowledge of ourselves. We find that everything exists because it has movement. Our ancestors understood the relationship between movement, space, time, and the life of us as humans. Nothing in the universe is in an absolute state or a finished state of perfection, it is an ongoing process.

This process we call "Ollin". Everything is in motion. When we understand and think like this we realize happiness, love, life and death are all cycles that give sense and shape to all things in existence. We must create because when we create, WE ARE!

This is why it is a challenge and an adventure for all of us. We must embark on this adventure to make it possible to find our happiness and our own destiny. We must try to do this for every moment of our lives. Will we accept this Challenge—maybe the biggest of our lives? If we can react calmly, then the challenge and the problems become exciting adventures. When we trust and have confidence to confront our problems and resolve them, we then have the knowledge, skill and the ability to overcome anything.

How can we do this? The answers we will find using the tools found herein.

What is "A Simple Truth?"

What if someone told us that we could feel connected, get a better understanding of the universe, feel and look healthier and understand our life's purpose, all this in twenty days? "A Simple Truth" is that book. This is the start of a journey for everyone, even for Luis and me as we write it. It is the words of the elders who shared the knowledge and taught the traditions through the years.

The day symbols are going to present things to us that are not part of some secret, for all knowledge already exists. We need only the keys to unlock the doors within our own minds to access it. This knowledge will help us all to find out our weaknesses and strengths, to work toward a better understanding of ourselves. The first thing is to really know who we are, and then we can work towards our destiny.

Most people have heard of, or know of a great stone calendar called the Aztec, Mayan or Sun calendar. They are all the same calendar, only the language is different.

The carving of this stone calendar was done fairly recently concerning history, but the calculations and information used for it were the culmination of thousands of years and generations of people versed in, and constantly studying the movement of the stars, planets and cycles on the Earth.

This book is not about the many facets of this great stone work, instead we are going to begin our adventure toward feeling connected with all that is, using the symbols that represent the day's signs found on this calendar.

This stone calendar has twenty day symbols, and these

symbols are located on one of the inner rings at the base
of the four cardinal points. They move in this inner ring in
a counter clockwise motion like some complex round slide
rule, recording time—both past and future.

The symbols are a key to understanding our physical experience, and a key that can give us the ability to feel how
we are creating and how we are a part of creation. This book
is for everyone who is trying to be more connected to all that
we know exists.

The twenty-day symbols are going to be presented to us in
an easy concept of the symbol. We must remember that these
suggestions are only part of a multi-layered symbol. These
symbols do not represent "Gods". These symbols have traits
found in their part of the natural world, and their existence.

Each chapter will share information about the days as
they are read on the calendar. At the end of each introduction
there will be exercises followed by a number of blank pages
to write responses. Therefore, by us responding to the questions and writing as much as we can, it is an opportunity for
us all to be a part of our study.

At the end, there will be some closing remarks to help us
better understand our "Tonalli" or destiny. Enjoy, relax, use
the key and step inside the door of a "Simple Truth".

Why A Simple Truth Now?

With so many changes occurring, this book is to help us all better understand what they mean, and also to give a better understanding of ourselves and the possibilities of what we can accomplish in these times. It is a simple truth. We need to "change" for all things do change and we can be in the flow with them, or we can butt heads against something that is going to happen anyway. This book will help us to change the things that need to be changed in our lives, and will give us an opportunity to walk in balance. Hopefully we'll find a place in our own families and communities where being more in balance can bring change within ourselves that benefits all.

Our lives are ephemeral, and this is the understanding that inspires us to do something important with them.

In the Nahuatl language, there is an expression, "In Xochitl In Kuikatl". Xochitl pronounced, "zoe-sheetl" means flower. This is in reference to the things we have created, the flowers. It can be the children, or those we mentor, our projects and the concrete things we have made. It could be a company, a school or buildings we helped to create. These are all flowers. Kuikatl pronounced, "Kwee-Cotl" means songs, our poetry, music, plans, these expressions of our ideas are songs we speak and share.

Our happiness and joy comes from our songs and flowers. With this book we encourage everyone to create beautiful flowers and beautiful songs. Though we leave behind the things we have made, by sharing this knowledge with others our songs and flowers will last forever.

Why Use the Symbols of the Aztec Calendar to Find Our Destiny?

If we begin to understand the concept of movement, then we can see that it creates cycles. There are cycles to the earth, the sun, the stars, the planets, nature, the seasons, the animals, plants, humans — everything has cycles…everything!

If we understand this concept of movement called "Ollin", then we begin to understand the relationship of everything and that the cycles in the universe are related to us because we are part of nature and creation.

This calendar makes it possible to understand the cycles of the earth and the universe. This calendar is the most accurate in the world because it is based on the movement of the stars, planets, moon and the seasons of the earth.

Even now it is used by hundreds of thousands of people in the counting of time. The calendar is not just the count of days or the counting of time; it is about how time directs our lives in the process of our existence. Time and space exist, they are not abstract concepts; this means they also are alive!

What Are the Symbols?

There are twenty-day symbols, used on the stone calendar. We will refer to this calendar as the Mexika calendar. However, this calendar was etched in stone under the instruction of a council that represented the area of Meso-America and beyond. Remember, they did not just start carving the stone; they had thousands of years of research and study of movement of the universe and our planet before they carved this great work.

All of this becomes something to further study, but for this book's purpose we are going to discuss only the twenty-day symbols.

These symbols represent things in the universe. They are part of creation but they are not gods. Because each symbol has multiple levels, we will try only to focus on the basics.

If you want to study further, you can contact us using the information at the end of this book to find out what is available to continue your journey.

How To Use This Book

As we begin, we are going to see the picture of the symbol (the pictures we are using are from the Codex Borgia.)

When we start to talk about this calendar we think it is just the count of time, but The Maya-Mexika Calendar was the basis of the existence of these societies. Even now in the Maya area for example this calendar still is in use by thousands.

The calendar is like an almanac about all movements including; time, space, stars, planets, the life of plants, animals, human beings. And the interrelationship between all of them. This calendar describes the cycles created from that interrelationship.

It gives us the knowledge, understanding, and confidence to be part of creation.

It is used to count time in a number of ways, but for our purposes we are going to use the count of 260—this is twenty months of thirteen days (Tonalpohualli).

This book is not the definitive book on the full meaning of the calendar or its symbols, but we will learn a different way to view and experience our physical time on this planet through a better understanding of these twenty symbols.

We use symbols every day in our lives and sometimes we do not even know the meaning of them. These 20 symbols carry the traits and characteristics of the human physical experience, and if we open our mind they will guide us on a journey of the universe, allowing us to grasp the vastness of the cosmos. Each symbol is part of everyone. Some may be more noticeable in you, but each has a place in all of us.

The knowledge to each symbol leads us to the next one. No symbol is more important than another. We must use all the symbols to complete the process. Try to have a goal to what we can accomplish in the twenty-day cycle. Do not try to make big projects or big changes until we are able to comprehend the meaning to each day's symbol. Only then will we be capable to use them in the right way to a higher purpose.

By doing the exercises, we will create our own journal that will guide us to complete our projects and excite us on this adventure. Turn the page and begin. This is Zipaktli.

Zipaktli

Crocodile

•

Ze

Day One

The first symbol, "Zipaktli" represents the origin. It is of the first medicine. It is day one. This is the beginning. No one knows exactly where this reptile form started, but it can be traced to a fossil that is at least 65 million years old. This was an animal that lived on land and in the water, was cold blooded and represents early life on this planet. We all started somewhere and this symbol represents our origin … where we began is a mystery. How far back can we go? The past is as infinite as the universe.

Zipaktli also represents conception, as in new life, and its form is also represented as love—the first emotion. This emotion is the start. We feel it from the beginning even in our mother's womb. We can also feel the absence of love even if we think we have never felt it, we can tell if it is missing.

Anything we can accomplish in life has a beginning, and in order to begin we must first stop—stop what we have been doing and start something new. As in meditation, we try to stop ourselves, clear our thoughts and minds. Then we can begin anew.

If we compare this concept to a ball that is bounced and reaches the top of its flight and is about to fall, the instant before it begins its descent, it stops—this is "Zipaktli". We already exist and the ball was thrown by Creator. How many times did it bounce before us? All of us have the capacity to create things and begin again at every moment.

We are constantly creating new things without thinking about it. Every second is a new start. Everything is constantly changing such as our cells renewing themselves. Everything outside and inside of us constantly changes. A caterpillar is a beautiful example of change, from walking the earth to flying through the air, but before it can fly it has to stop and start anew. With its cocoon it stops, and then begins again.

We must begin with something somewhere. We think in terms of time. We realize we have the capacity to stop and begin, this is Zipaktli.

Exercises

(Use the following pages after each symbol for your answers.)

• Is it easy for you to start new things? If it is not, what stops you from doing it? List your reasons.

• If it is easy for you to start things, what have you started and where are you in the things you started. Have you finished your projects?

• Let's start something, think of something you wanted to start and felt unable to do. Now we begin!!

Worksheet

Worksheet

Worksheet

Ehekatl

Wind

• •

Ome

Day Two

The breath of life is the Spirit or Soul for most cultures around the world since the origin of civilization, "Ehekatl" represents the breath of life.

We come from an environment of water. Now we take in the first breath and breathe oxygen, our planet's air.

First we have our origin (Zipaktli) and then we begin to breath. When we take our first breath we think we are dying. We are aware that things have changed now we breathe air it is new and we cry, this is the manifestation of our existence. Think about how every breath is as important as that first one, how our body tells us to breathe. Each breath could be our last if we do not take another. We live separately from our mothers now.

The wind is what spreads the seeds that make all of life possible. Its movement also keeps things from becoming stagnant. It refreshes and circulates around us all of the time. What motivates us to start to do something—anything? What force makes the movement of the leaves in the trees, and what makes the seed come from the ground? Something makes it possible for things to move. Not the movement itself, but the thing that made it possible is an example of Ehekatl.

The first breath is our first meal. It is the first thing we take in as nourishment. It feeds us for the rest of our lives. Ehekatl makes movement possible but not just on the earth. It inspires us and it pushes us along with everything.

The wind is something we see when a tree moves, and we feel the effect of it on our skin, but we can't hold it in our hands. We see its effects but cannot actually see it.

We can hear it in the sound of nature like the songs from the birds, our voices, different languages, and music in our hearts. We sense it in the breeze blowing thru the trees, the waves of the sea, the buzz of insects, smell, light, heat and even the cold is possible to perceive because of Ehekatl. In fact, silence itself doesn't exist; even the quietest places have noises.

Ehekatl is the essence to keep us alive.

Exercises

• Do you push yourself to do things?

• In doing things are you giving thought to this process, or are you just doing them?

• What really moves you and inspires you to do different things?

Worksheet

Worksheet

Worksheet

Kalli

House

• • •

Yei

Day Three

"Kalli" represents the house. We began somewhere (Zipaktli); we are breathing (Ehekatl), and now we need somewhere to live—the house. This symbol is where we live, but also it is the body or home we inhabit physically, our temple. When you look at your house/body does it have a good foundation? Is it in a good place? Is it in balance?

This symbol doesn't just represent the house. It also represents our own space. It is not just the place we call home but it is also all that we are surrounding ourselves with including the environment we create in this place in time. No matter where we've started, at some point in our lives, we must take responsibility for where we are now, and then start from there.

This symbol also represents a point to start from. We are the ones who have the will and power to change anything, including ourselves. No one can do this for us. We fix our own house, our surroundings and our environment. If it needs anything, we are the starting point. We ultimately are responsible for fixing our homes. Maybe just by putting plants in our home, having good eating habits etc. It is "our" house, this is very important to remember. We all have a place we call home. Love your home and take care of it. It is our temple. It is sacred. Treat it with respect. It helps us to reflect, and home is where we go to be safe, so it needs to be a place of harmony.

Right after our motivation, we have the realization of our environment. We are creating our own environment; this is where we get the tools for our development and realize, "I belong to this place" and that we create our walls, our nest, or whatever we call home. When we have our own place, we feel safe, protected, warmth, and secure.

Look at the animals and how they build their houses, nests, dens…their homes. Everything needs its own space to survive. We return to our Kalli to feel secure. When we create our space, we should feel good about it. Even nests, dens, and some holes in the ground are places created to make its occupants feel at home. When children draw on walls they are trying to create their own space. Animals mark their territory or place they consider to be their home.

All of this is our home, so we should treat it with respect and let it be something we look forward to.

Exercises

• Our physical body is our home. How do you see yours, and how can you improve it?

• Do you like your home—the place you are living—not just the location, but the ones who live with you and around you? What can you do to improve your surroundings? Where is a good place to start?

• Do you ever go home? If so, how many times a year and what did you do the last time you went "home"?

Worksheet

Worksheet

Worksheet

Kuetzpallin

Lizard

• • • •

Naui

Day Four

We all begin, we are breathing and we are creating our environment. Where do we get our energy? The fourth symbol, "Kuetzpallin", is another entity around us that has been here longer than humans. It is cold blooded but most importantly it absorbs the energy from the sun. Since the lizard is cold blooded, in the morning it sits very still on a rock in the sun, and then once the lizard is warmed up it starts moving.

The sun is the reason we can exist here on this planet, in this place in the universe; the sun is exactly where it needs to be for us to live here. For how long…that is up to us. We can alter the time that our planet is habitable because we are humans. As part of creation, we humans also draw energy and nutrition from the sun.

Open your hands. As the sun rises over the horizon expose your palms to the sun and raise them up high. You will feel the energy of the sun. When the days get shorter and there is not a lot of sunlight it affects us and how we act.

"Kuetzpallin" represents nourishment and that is what causes us to move. We think nourishment is some-times only food, but what helped the food to grow? The sun,the same thing that causes the lizard to move. The lizard represents the way we transform nourishment into movement.

We truly are what we eat. In most cultures, their pri-mary nourishment is an important symbol. For some humans, it is corn and we see it in ancient symbols because of that importance, but *all* things need the energy of the sun. No matter where they are, the places we do not even think of, they all receive this energy.

Kuetzpallin is a symbol to movement, but also a start of finding out about cycles that happen in getting our nourishment such as plants growing and their harvest, but it is also about understanding the movement in our cycles. We develop and start to realize we and all things are sexual.

Here we must respect what we eat and develop good eating habits. Nourishment is not only our food it is the energy that created it. We transform this energy in our bodies to begin to move. We must know that all things move because of this transfer of energy of the sun. In short, this symbol is a representation of rejuvenation or a starting to move on things that we left stagnant.

Exercises

• Make a list of how you start your day. Then make a list of how you would like to start your day.

• Do you consider yourself an energetic person or do you need something to get you started?

• Are you able to sustain your energy for the entire day? How do you keep it?

Worksheet

Worksheet

Worksheet

Kuetzpallin

Serpent

—

Makuilli

Day Five

The serpent "Koatl," is misunderstood. By many, the serpent is thought of as sneaky and not the most trusted. The snake lives under things, underground and under rocks. It can slow its metabolism and it hibernates. The serpent's movement is similar to a sine wave showing the pulse of electrical current.

Koatl represents intelligence because in its movement, it always finds the easiest way, and by doing this it shows intelligence. The serpent moves effortlessly without arms or legs. The serpent never butts heads with an object or obstacle—it always goes around.

The serpent represents the knowledge; things that we can learn to tap into it. We start to believe the thoughts from our minds. We start to understand that knowledge is all around us, and we must move in synch with it.

Throughout history in the great societies, all of those who built the pyramids used the serpent as the entry point for those who would study the knowledge. You usually entered thru the serpent's mouth. These were the ones who taught the mathematics or anything we would consider science related.

This symbol means starting to plan our itinerary, our next move in our life. To make an itinerary we have to think about what we want to do. By using our senses to achieve our goals, we define intelligence. It means learning to not butt heads, but to go around obstacles and shed our old skin. Make our movement seem effortless. If we are on the right path it will be effortless.

The serpent represents not just spoken intelligence but also in the way we move. Physically the serpent is very sensitive; it hears, smells and tastes the space it occupies when it sticks its tongue out. After it evaluates its place, it knows where it will move.

The serpent teaches us how to see our feelings in the best way; in order to do what we want to. The serpent knows when it is confronted and when it can move away. It recognizes the shortest way to achieve its goal. The serpent with no arms or legs is more sensitive to its surroundings than we are. Isn't this intelligence? We move with our feelings, and feel through our senses. This is "Koatl".

Exercises

• Do you butt heads or do you go around obstacles in your life? How do you confront those situations in your life?

• Do you have a plan to resolve the situations that come up in your life? Write about what that plan would look like.

• Are you stuck having the same thoughts? How can you change your way of thinking and use your mind differently?

Worksheet

Worksheet

Worksheet

Mikiztli

Death

•

Chikoazen

Day Six

"Mikiztli" is generally called death because the symbol is shown as a skull. It stands though, for transformation. We receive knowledge and we transform it into something for our life's purpose. We can transform into a new person at any moment. Sometimes the plans of our itinerary get changed and we're stuck in our ways. We need to change, break routine and transform ourselves. Death is just another trans-formation from the physical to the spiritual, but this symbol isn't about death but about transforming and being reborn while still alive. We become ancestors, we are the continuity to those who came before us and we lead the way for those who come after us. We constantly transform, this also is a symbol of rejuvenation. It is here that we evaluate what is life and death.

Mikiztli shows the skull with circles and flowers on it. The flowers are because we are still influencing the ones who come after us even after we've transformed. After we leave the physical our spirit or soul becomes blended into the universe, the stars, the space between them, and the make-up of all that exists. We become those stars and the night sky.

When we think of those who have gone before us we usually look up, not down. We look to the universe and won-der how our loved ones are doing. In our minds we know that they have transformed. We do not have the physical person to interact with but we have the memories that suddenly will make us laugh or cry.

These are real feelings brought about because of someone whether they are here with us at this time or not. They may not be physically here but our minds bring them here in a flash.

If we don't like where we are, we can transform ourselves to become better people. Do something different than we would normally do. We can transform anything, but first we must start with ourselves. It's time to look at the things we have made and the things we still need to make. Nothing dies until we lose the memory of it.

Why is it that we sometimes do not appreciate life until we are confronted with our mortality, for instance? If someone today told you that you have one month to live, you will suddenly start to want to live. We should live every day as if we just received that news. Every day cells die and new ones come, so we are constantly transforming, though most people are unaware of that transformation. When we really think about it, we are only here on the earth for an instant. We must live our lives with this appreciation. Transform ourselves into someone we really like, and we will be happy.

Exercises

• Are you afraid of death? Explain your fear.

• What changes are you afraid of making? Make a list.

• Are you keeping the good things alive in your life? Make a list of the good things and bring them back to life.

Worksheet

Worksheet

Worksheet

Mazatl

Deer

..

Chikome

Day Seven

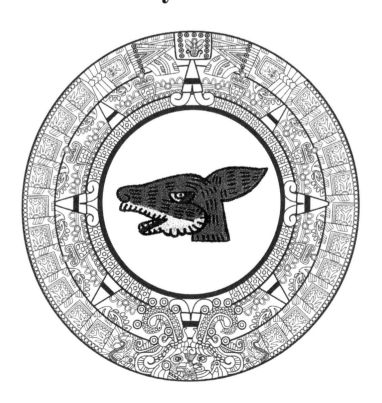

At this point we are now transforming knowledge, forming our own personalities and beginning to form our thoughts. "Mazatl" is the symbol that we learn sensitivity and intuition from. The deer is so sensitive it can feel vibrations in the ground through its feet. This symbol is also related to our ESP, insight as well as intuition. The deer is very aware of things in its environment. The deer has exceptional hearing and it is fast, agile and graceful. It chooses a path carefully. When it is born, it has spots to protect and conceal it from things that would cause it harm.

A deer can survive in the desert and is one of only a few mammals that can. They are the teacher's of how to survive. What this symbol means to us is to use our emotions and intuition; in this way we really listen to people. Our instincts will protect us, teach us how to survive and show us how to choose our path. We are responsible for the path we have chosen...we cannot blame others.

We choose carefully where we are headed because we realize that life is all about choices and paths.

Mazatl also represents restlessness and quick change. We become aware of things that happen in our environment all around us.

Mazatl is about perception. We start to understand our instincts, feelings and emotions; listening to them, we learn a better understanding of our lives. This helps us to be more aware.

The perception of a feeling comes to us through our sensitivity, and each person's perception is different. With this sensitivity we can better understand ourselves and everything around us.

We can then have an awareness and sensitivity that allows us to quickly react and choose the right way to go. Improve our sensitivity and we learn to react quickly in the best way.

Instead of fearing or being overcome by these feelings and emotions, we must learn to understand them with a sensitivity that can guide us in choosing our path.

Exercises

• Do you find yourself talking more than listening?

• Do you use your instincts and feelings? Are you aware what they are telling you?

• Make a list of your feelings and then write down your experiences where you used your intuition.

Worksheet

Worksheet

Worksheet

Tochtli

Rabbit

. . .

Chikuei

Day Eight

"Tochtli" represents fertility and the ability to create in abundance. Humanity is multiplying, and we are part of this expanding universe. We are "Tochtli". We see all things as part of our community; we are able to create, but we have no purpose yet and do not fully know our place in our communities. When we are children we don't think of ourselves as separate from our parents. So being separate is a learned behavior. But now as we grow and mature through the awakening process, we find that the children were right ... we are all connected!

Mazatl *shows* us the path and Tochtli teaches us to *follow* the path. Tochtli also represents pleasure and harmony. We cultivate our abilities to help what we feel is our community. The rabbit is related to the moon and follows the cycles. It creates life in one cycle of the moon (gestation for rabbits is 28 days). Rabbits have the same rhythm and cycles as humans, and we also are affected by the moon.

Something pushes to keep all species alive. This is a survival instinct. How is this done? All species create others like them. We are following the path that creation gives us. The path is to follow the cycles in nature, in ourselves, and in all things.

We follow our instincts most of the time and Tochtli is about following those instincts. Why do we sleep at night? 'Because of our instincts. We do not really think about it but we do it. Tochtli represents the cycles already in our lives and we do things instinctively with-

out thinking about them. When we mature, we hopefully do think before we react.

We follow the cycles in nature whether we are aware
of them or not. We know when it is time to plant, or time
to harvest the crops. We know when to prepare for the
change in the seasons. We do things prior to the changes
in these cycles. This is "Tochtli". If we become more
aware of the cycles in nature we learn how to live using
our instincts in their best way, and we can create with
purpose.

Exercises

• Are you aware about the cycles in nature and yourself?
Write down cycles you are aware of.

• Are you aware of the difference between instincts and
feelings? Name some things that are instinctual.

• Do you feel you have a path and are creating using
the natural cycles in your life?

Worksheet

Worksheet

Worksheet

Atl

Water

....

Chiknaui

Day Nine

We follow our instincts, we now have tools to create, but we need "Atl" to give those things life. Nothing exists without this element. It represents our life blood for we cannot live without water. We are made up of 70% water. We might not need food but we need water. Water is the element needed for all life on this planet.

We now can create life but must think how we will sustain it. It is impossible to understand ourselves without knowing that water is what sustains all that lives on earth. Water is the most important element because it is life. The woman's womb has the water of life in it. We can have energy from the sun, but without water, we cannot live. When NASA sends their missions to space, the first thing they are looking for is water, not people or plants.

Water must be respected because it is something we must allow to flow. There is only so much water that humans can use and survive. Water must remain in motion or it becomes no good. That is why Atl is a symbol helping us to understand respect. Without respect for all of the elements we lose our life. With respect we can understand the value of all things.

We are like water in a constant motion of creativity and movement. The force of water can be controlled in only a few circumstances.

Water can be calm and comforting in the bathtub but in the ocean it can kill us. Even in a tub it can kill us.

We must respect the water in the tub for it has the same value as the water in the ocean.

Everything has value and we need to fully appreciate this. We mostly respect things if we think they are good, or we will respect them if we think they can harm or kill us, but everything has its value and place on the planet.

We must respect all things because they all have value and we sometimes do not think about it. Water can teach us respect because by understanding it we can appreciate the value in all things.

We are connected with everything through water for it is what makes life possible. In all traditions water is sacred. We sometimes do not realize this connection to everything.

Although Atl, water and respect are simple words, if we really think about them, they teach us to give value to everything.

Exercises

• What do you know about the elements? Do you know their importance, especially water?

• When we realize the value of water we respect it. Can you apply this respect to everything? What do you value?

• How are your actions demonstrating your respect for all things? How can you improve them?

Worksheet

Worksheet

Worksheet

Itzkuintli

Dog

=

Matlaktli

Day Ten

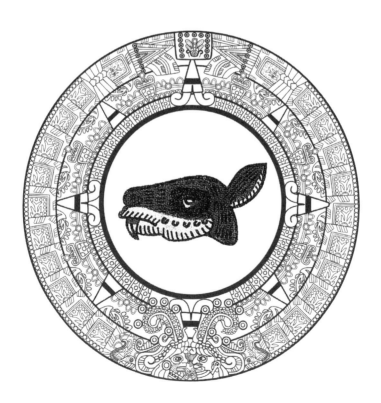

We now know Atl keeps us alive, and we realize respect is needed for everything. So what is "Itzkuintli" doing here? The dog is the first domesticated animal and it is very adaptable. The dog lives best in a community and it realizes its purpose and fulfills that role in the community. We all relate to the dog and can adapt to roles in our communities.

Sometimes we are raised in ways that never fulfill our real roles. Itzkuintli shows us how to find our role. A dog will not complain, and remains loyal and dedicated to its community. It shows us unconditional love. Dogs are sent out of the community and are ostracized if they act in a bad way.

Dogs have great strength and perseverance. They do not forget where they come from. They find their way home. They protect their community and mark their territory (the space that is our territory to create what we want.) The house is where we start. The dog is where we go out to do our "thing". We start to realize actions that take risks or are instincts and use this evaluation in our relationships with others. The dog can guide us or be our partner. It likes to make new friends and visit other places but always returns home.

We are starting to understand that we belong to a community and that we do not do things by ourselves. We need others. The first community is the family. Today though, in our current society, we find ourselves alone most of the time; even knowing we need others to really accomplish the best things we are capable of producing.

We do not have our families as close as they once were and most of us do not foster community around us. This is an important lesson to learn from Itzkuintli—we need others and the people we find around us are our family. We need to find a way to work together with them.

As we start to learn our role and purpose in the community, we can start to fulfill it. We will protect and support our communities and be able to work together with others. We have learned about respect, now we are learning about loyalty to our community. We are ready now to protect the things that we love and when we have this loyalty, we will be ready to do anything to protect our goals and the goals of our family and community.

Exercises

• Write down what you think your role and purpose is in your family and communities.

• Do you really have ties with your family and community? If yes, describe those ties.

• Are you still creating new ties using perseverance and loyalty? What do these words mean to you?

Worksheet

Worksheet

Worksheet

Ozomahtli

Monkey

Matlaktli Iuan Ze

Day Eleven

"Ozomahtli" represents skills and abilities. Now we need the ability to grasp the things Creator has set before us and find out what our skills and abilities are. The monkey lives in a community and takes care of and helps its neighbors. They care for each other and will even groom each other. The monkey is able to grasp with its tail, hands and feet. The tail is considered the fifth hand.

We start to grasp things and gain the ability to hold on to them. This means by grasping concepts and theories, we gain a better understanding of our capabilities. We need to find our special talents and skills and use them to find our destiny or tonalli in life. Sometimes someone has talent to play the piano but their parents never gave them piano lessons so they don't know it yet. Ozomahtli is where we find our artistic talents and develop our perspectives of sensuality.

We associate Ozomahtli with creative elements of plants and food and the making of it. This is where we learn skills but also how we play and have recreation. Our abilities and skills are already ingrained in us. Like us, monkeys have hands and use tools and the hands relate to skills and creativity. Monkeys have a system of communication and a reference to humans but their hands are similar to their feet.

We understand that we all have different skills and abilities, but must develop them. When we find things that we are good at, we must pursue them and we will find pleasure. Monkeys enjoy who they are and what they are doing.

When we find what we are good at, we have to grasp it and hold onto it with everything. Our hands are how we create. We can create new and different skills. We have the ability to learn new skills because we grow as we learn them.

When we feel we are able to really grasp something and do it, we will be happy. But we must really show it and express it. If we haven't found what makes us happy yet, we shouldn't be sad. We develop different skills throughout our entire lives. We find something else that we desire and find joy and happiness in the creation of it. We must realize and recognize our real skills and abilities and then go for it. Remember, we always have the ability to learn.

Exercises

• Have you grasped what your special talents and abilities are? Write them down.

• Do you believe these really are your skills and abilities, or are you feeling like there is something else you can or should do? What are you doing about it?

• Are you really holding onto your talents and grasping them with all that you have? How can you really enjoy what you are good at?

Worksheet

Worksheet

Worksheet

Malinalli

Vines

Matlaktli Iuan Ome

Day Twelve

"Malinalli" is said to be the weeds or vines but it is also the symbol that represents the interrelationship with nature and all the beings. It is about us learning to interweave with nature. Here we start learning about the natural world and how we are a part of it. This is about the interconnectedness of all that exists, and our place in it. Nature is where we get our nourishment. We are one with nature.

We are part of the weave! We create all things from nature and this weave also represents society. In Mexico, in a traditional indigenous wedding, the couple sits on a woven mat called a "petate", and it is to show us our tie to all that exists, and also to remind us that marriage is the interweaving of two lives.

Knowing the interconnectedness of everything, we do not feel alienated from nature; instead we can feel more balanced knowing we are part of it. Our correct interaction with nature helps us to help others. We can learn the medicine of the herbs and how to use them in maintaining health for ourselves and everything around us. There are many ways in which we humans interact with nature some make baskets from roots found in the ground, others create new materials from the same thing, "NATURE". All of this is our connection and interaction with nature.

Most people do not realize we are nature! This is not a slogan, but is the truth. We are a part of all that exists on the earth. We have roots, we are the earth.

The life that exists on earth is part of nature, not separated, and this interrelationship and the soil from which all things grow is Malinalli.

The soil produces our nourishment and it is made from everything that has gone before us. It becomes part of us. Our bodies need minerals, iron, zinc, potassium, etc. Where do they come from? From our food and where does it come from?

The best teacher is in nature, and so we learn how to utilize the plants and animals on the earth. We are the earth. We come from it, but we are still just a part of it. When we say, "Mother Earth" we acknowledge our relationship to it and how important that connection is.

Humans do not rule over nature, rather we are supposed to be the part of Creation that helps keep it in balance. We are starting to work towards improving our environment and becoming more in balance with it.

Exercises

• Do you feel connected with nature? If so, how?

• How can you improve your connection and understanding of nature?

• With this understanding of nature, how are you working to restore the balance? What will you do?

Worksheet

Worksheet

Worksheet

Akatl

Reed

Matlaktli Iuan Yei

Day Thirteen

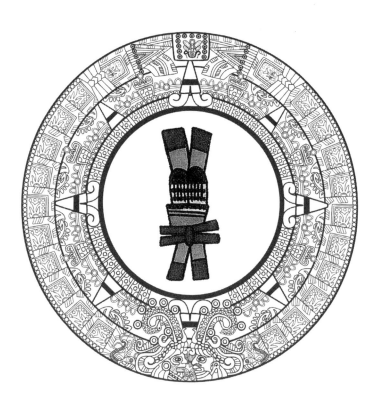

"Akatl" is associated with time. Like the bamboo reed, it is segmented by a knot and each section represents a period of time. Akatl is about how we grow and how time affects us.

We are growing older and we recognize the past, yet we can start a new period of our life at any time. We are all passing through time, even as we read these words everything thus far has become the past. What is behind us goes back forever but the present is only for the moment. We must appreciate time and try to use it in the best way possible.

At the same time Akatl is about the analysis, observation and awareness of building stable and constructive projects with effective plans. The sections represent segments in terms of time in our lives and planned goals.

When we start to think deeply we get more understanding and think more philosophically. Time, and the realization of it, is deep. When we see things growing we may not observe their growth or them getting older in the moment, but they are. We use the reed because we can clearly see the change. We analyze this and see how time has passed.

We can see time in all things and record what has happened. Like the seasons and knowing when it is time to plant, we start projects and we learn how to improve them and continue them by understanding the time that has passed. We use the knowledge we call experience to improve our ideas and actions.

When we understand this process we can create things and achieve our goals knowing each part of this process is time. We must start projects but we also must complete them. We create our plans based on time.

Time is not an invention made by humans, it is a fact. Perception of time is measured differently according to us as individuals, but also by everything else; the plants, animals and insects. All things on our planet measure time according to their existence—we live around eighty years, the gnat lives only a day, the turtle lives over a hundred years or the red wood forest that lives hundreds of years. Time and life are relevant to everything.

When we learn the relationship of time and our movement with it, we gain knowledge and experience from the past and create a future using time in the best way.

Exercises

• Do you always worry about the future and forget to live in the moment?

• Do you finish projects and goals when you say you will? If so, do you do it on time?

• Make a schedule of your usual day, examine this and ask yourself if you are using your time well. How can you improve it and make it enjoyable?

Worksheet

Worksheet

Worksheet

Ozelotl

Ocelot

Matlaktli Iuan Naui

Day Fourteen

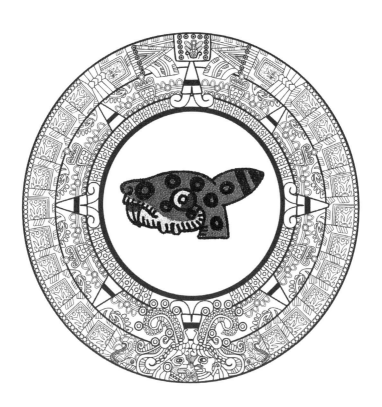

This is an animal of the night. "Ozelotl" is about darkness and depth. The Ozelotl is covered with spots and stripes. The spots represent the stars and the stripes, the milky way. When we see the stars in the sky at night it connects us with the universe and so does this symbol.

Ozelotl also represents the darkest caves and places beneath the earth. We are not just part of space; we are part of all that has come before us and everything around us and beneath us.

Ozelotl is seen only when we really look and concentrate to see it. We can walk right past one without knowing it. To see the Ozelotl, we must look for it, and in the same way we must really look and think deeply and cultivate abstract thoughts about everything around us. We can search and find answers not just to things easily revealed. The Ozelotl lives in the night, is agile, hunts for food at night and is comfortable in the darkness.

Ozelotl represents our ability to understand the universe. We know the spots relate to the stars and the darkness as the space between. We are realizing that we are part of the universe. We can think of universal time now. We want to contribute to the next generation. We are trying to understand the universe and it is represented by darkness because it is so vast, so deep and yet we can think of its depth. We begin to understand its vastness but it takes a life time to really study it.

We look at the stars and think how we are, and how vast the universe is. In the darkness we cannot realize the boundaries of the space we are in. If we are in a room and it is dark, we do not know the size of the room. The same if we are outside in the darkness, we do not think about its boundaries. When we lie down and look up at the stars we see them as part of the universe.

This knowledge made possible the creation of the Mexika calendar, the most accurate calendar on the planet. The people who left this calendar for us understood the universe before anyone else. They were able to predict the eclipses and other events with their awareness of astronomy. The ancestors of this calendar studied the stars and planets for thousands of years, and we receive the benefit of that study. They studied the sky and the movement of objects and marked the time it took them to return to the recorded place. The stars on this symbol represent the night and are shown as eyes. We say the stars are the witness of time because they were here before us and will be here after us.

With Ozelotl we can understand the universe and our relationship with it. We have a role in it.

There is a reason for us in the universe. When we want to do something we have to think in terms of the universe. We can create great things that reach beyond us or our communities. We can create really large things. All that happens in the universe affects us in some way.

Exercises

• We said the light from the stars connects us to our past; how do you think that is?

• What kind of goals do you set for yourself? Can you reach higher? What do you really want to do? What would you be? Do you know why you are here?

• Do you think about things deeply? Are you able to analyze? Think and answer this question: What does thirteen multiplied by twenty equal? Is this just a question of math or is it a formula? Does it relate to us? How does it?

Worksheet

Worksheet

Worksheet

Kuauhtli

Eagle

≡

Kachtoli

Day Fifteen

The eagle flies higher than any other bird, it is said that "Kuauhtli" can reach the top of the sky. It has the greatest vision, it can see for miles and miles. Maybe we can get a perception of this vision if it can be explained as one who had the vision to land people on the moon, or that we could make things fly and pilot them. This is Kuauhtli. It represents the human being. If it can be thought, it can be created. Do not underestimate the things humans can create or have created.

When we look deeply and thoroughly into nature, the stars, a sunset or even our meals, we sense our connection and feel it as part of us. This is real and this is the essence of our spirituality.

To have the sensation of tenderness toward an elder, a child or the littlest things like a firefly in the night, this is Kuauhtli. This feeling or vision gives us respect for others; even a bug, a weed or a place. Others can think of things in different ways, and we have to accept and respect those differences. When we judge others we listen only to ourselves.

Kuauhtli can see what's coming in front of it. We get clear vision with the ability to rise above all things. We find clarity, gain greater perception for our lives and it becomes clear where we're headed. We start to feel spiritually connected to creation.

We can see and feel ourselves as part of everything. We value and respect our elders because this symbol represents our elders.

Elders present their knowledge this way because they have the vision of a life lived. This means they have a broad vision of everything around them, but we do not always have to be old to have this vision.

Kuauhtli is where we form our tonalli because we realize where we are and the things we can do for ourselves and others. We can   think about the next generations and we understand the lessons we have learned in this life. We can understand what we are, who we are and how we can achieve our tonalli. We are maturing in all aspects of our life.

Our point of view of spirit is only our perception. The idea of a Creator is unique as to the perceiver. Everything in nature has a perception of its existence. We cannot insist we are more spiritual than someone or something else. We must respect other beliefs. We have a broad vision and we are able to live better lives using it, but we also help others by our example—this is spiritual—this is Kuauhtli.

Exercises

• Are you starting to see more clearly? List the things you see differently.

• Do you respect different points of views? List some experiences with other religions other than what you consider to be your own.

• What is spirituality to you?

Worksheet

Worksheet

Worksheet

Kozkakuauhtli

Condor

Kachtoli Iuan Ze

Day Sixteen

"Kozkakuautli", the condor, we relate to as the eagle with the necklace or collar. This is a bird that is similar to the vulture of today, but for the calendar it was the condor that it was modeled after.

What can we learn from this symbol? This is an animal that doesn't kill for its food. It eats dead things. It makes use of what others see no value in or are no longer seen as useful to them.

Kozkakuautli shows us a way to reinterpret things and have a vision for the future in things others don't see. It is the recycler. It soars for hours without using any of its energy. It can reflect and consider its actions. It flies with the wind and is one of the largest flyers.

Kuautli (eagle) helps us to find our Tonalli (destiny) but Kozkakuautli helps us to be able to do what we must do to achieve our destiny and do it in the best way. The condor has an important role in nature. It eats dead animals in order to survive. This is valuable because others won't even try to eat dead things.

Our lives do not always go the way we think and Kozkakuautli helps us to go with the wind in the correct direction. Some of us do things that no one else will or can do, but we do them even though it could be distasteful in order to survive. Kozkakuautli can give us the capacity to analyze the usefulness of things around us.

Our opportunity can be in front of us though we may not see it. This symbol allows us to have vision to see things in a different way. We can have the knowledge that we do not even know we have. Sometimes we can learn from others that are considered slow or not so intelligent. They may have knowledge to resolve our questions even though they think differently. We have to think and reevaluate the way we see things in our lives.

We learn that things that have passed or are behind us offer a real value. Even what we consider a missed opportunity can give us experience and help us understand our lives.

Kozkakuauhtli uses things but does not keep them. We should not use our energy on keeping things. We must use things and move on. This helps us to take our time to see the value of things and then to pass that along, but Kozkakuauhtli also knows when the best opportunity is upon them to use something. The key is to find a way to use opportunity and recognize it. People who have this vision usually can teach others.

Exercises

• Do you find value in things others would discard? What kind of things?

• Have you ever had to do something you did not want to do but had to because no one else would? What was it?

• What opportunities have passed you by? Describe those experiences.

Worksheet

Worksheet

Worksheet

Ollin

Movement

Kaxtoli Iuan Ome

Day Seventeen

"Ollin" represents movement or action. We have some things now to help find our life's purpose. We now must act. We must do something that is ours. We must work for it and with the people. We must find our destiny in our tonalli.

This symbol reminds us that everything is in motion. Everything! We need ideas and inspiration. Movement is a fundamental attribute of all matter. Things are solid because they have movement. We need to move and act on our destiny. Tiahui in the Nahautl language means forward but it encourages us to move ahead.

Movement is like the waves in the ocean being not always the same; sometimes many or few, big or small, fast or slow. Movement is different to each thing, like the turtle or the gazelle, some things we see right away, but most of the time we do not notice. Ollin is the relationship of movement between all things.

Was our universe created and that was it, or is it still going on? Creation is still going on and we are all alive and moving, and part of it.

We can see our actions. We consider them and make wise decisions. More than just action, we have to have action with intent and ideas. We are doing things in a correct way to accomplish our goals. We think now toward the movement of things, but even into the future we think in a transcendental way about all things, even for the next generation, even beyond our own lives. We may start projects knowing they will take more time than we have, but we will go for it. We will start things forward, this is Ollin.

We find most of our great projects happen because of the involvement of others. It can be our communities, families, or anybody around us, but it usually involves others. Our actions benefit our families, communities, and the projects we have begun. Like saving the rain forest or saving the whales, projects that get others involved helping, and this is Ollin. Now we have to get moving, we have to do something, act on something.

Exercises

• Are you a person of action? Explain either way.

• Are you in the process of achieving your goals in life? Do you use a method to achieve your goals?

• Once you have figured out your life's purpose how can you act on it? What will your next move be?

Worksheet

Worksheet

Worksheet

Tekpatl

Flint

Kaxtoli Iuan Yei

Day Eighteen

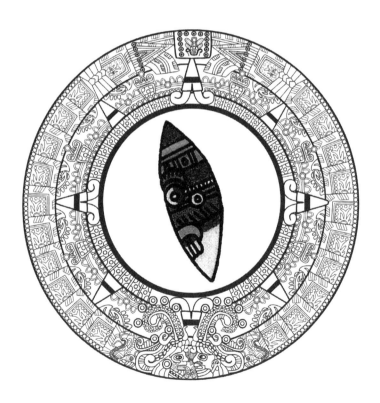

"Tekpatl" is the flint, the spark to sharpen our skills and purpose. We get our ideas, like the sparks from a flint. We work on those ideas that keep coming to our minds and we start working on them through sharing them with others. This is the flint, this is stone, but it needs something to strike it to inspire it. We hone our skills and use them with others.

We are able to comprehend great ideas and work towards achieving them. We are accepting help from others who have been inspired because our ideas pierce into their thoughts and begin to inspire them. Tekpatl creates the ideas and these ideas are the wisdom we have gained from our experience.

This wisdom can create social, political, environmental or any kind of movement because it inspires everyone. Tekpatl represents the knowledge to bring forth ideas in a good way and inspires people to support our ideas and create more. We show this through sharing our knowledge and actions.

When we begin to create our projects, the community and people around us through their involvement, help to make other ideas. Tekpatl is our inspiration to motivate others by our example.

When we are moving towards something, we get our ideas and inspire others. We have the ability to cut through our fears and achieve our goals.

Martin Luther King Jr. had a dream and was able to

inspire society even after he was gone. He was able to pierce into the consciousness of society and deeply affect people in a way so they became inspired by his actions. This is an example of Tekpatl.

Sometimes we can read a book, or listen to someone, or see something that changes our whole life. We inspire others by our thoughts, words and actions. A scientist, Thomas Alva Edison, made hundreds of inventions and one of them was a spark; we see it in the lights in our homes today. And also author, William Shakespeare, whose words are spoken on stages everywhere today, along with Mahatma Gandhi whose actions inspired millions of people to find their freedom without violence. His actions still inspire millions today. These are examples of Tekpatl.

When we do things in a good way our example becomes the inspiration for others, our ideas inspire others and their ideas inspire, and so on.

Exercises

• Do you work with others and share ideas? Name some projects that you have led or done with others.

• Name people who have inspired you or you have inspired, and in what way?

• How are you acting to inspire others and make them be a part of your ideas?

Worksheet

Worksheet

Worksheet

Kiauitl

Rain

Kachtoli Iuan Naui

Day Nineteen

We have the spark; now the ideas rain down on us when we have found our life's purpose. We can have dreams in abundance. There are so many raindrops we can't count them, we cannot stand between them, they shower us repeatedly. This is "Kiauitl", it makes dreams come true, it helps things grow, it replenishes that which is dried up and it cleanses the things it rains on.

Kiauitl means starting fresh projects using all of the process that has brought us to this point. We are receiving ideas and choosing the ones we connect with all the time. Working with others or alone, we can feel when we are overwhelmed, and we know when to seek shelter to get out of the rain. We know when we need to water our ideas so they can grow.

We are in the process of creating and making valuable things, but in order to construct our Tonalli we do not just need the plans, we need other elements around us as they come together to create our Tonalli. For example, a tree needs the soil, the sun, the rain and so many more things. How many things come together to make a house, the plumbing, framing, wiring, roofing, landscaping, and painting; all these different things create some part, and again these are not the only things … there are many others. What about the sun, a star, our planet; how many things make these exist? We cannot count them. This is Kiauitl.

We evaluate when we need more rain, or less, and put ourselves in the place that we can get what we need.

We have the ability to have many projects. We are not just one idea, we are many things. We must work to create things in abundance. To find our destiny, we receive the teachings and ideas of many. We use these ideas to develop our communities, our environments and ourselves. We realize that to accomplish our goals, it involves many people.

"A Simple Truth" could be a good example because it comes from the teachings of our ancestors. It comes from ancient knowledge that has been interpreted by the authors, by our friends and through real, meaningful and life changing experiences. When we apply it in our lives, this knowledge will become our destiny. We all receive something that will benefit ourselves.

Through these pages there is something for everyone. All of us have our own experience and perception of what that is, and this is Kiauitl. We are many things. Do not think we are only one. Create many things.

Exercises

• Are you in a period of your life where you know your life's purpose and are ideas raining down on you? What are they?

• How can you use the ideas you are receiving to help you and others to grow?

• Now, list some thoughts you have but haven't yet shared.

Worksheet

Worksheet

Worksheet

Xochitl

Flower

•

Zempoalli

Day Twenty

"Xochitl" (true happiness, our Tonalli, our destiny) is what we are all trying to achieve. Do not stop with only one goal or one task, but be prolific and create a lot of bouquets with different flowers. Enjoy the fragrance from them, feeling the powerful and spiritual sensation from those things created from each of us.

After the creation of our flower, that flower doesn't belong just to us. Everybody will be able to feel, smell and see Xochitl!

We will be willing to understand and learn about that flower, but also the essence from us will stay in Xochitl, like the Mona Lisa from Leonardo Da Vinci, a book, the house where we live, even the little things like a small seed. In all things the creator of them will be living in some way, even after the creator of these special things has transformed.

In the same way, we must take care of those beautiful flowers. They need attention and care because only when we understand the value and importance to these flowers do they become Xochitl.

The blossom of the flower is us in our prime. When we are the most productive, we use all of our knowledge, abilities, qualities and talents. We fulfill our destiny and produce beautiful things by our materialized acts. Sometimes it is our life's work, or the people around us, or our children. All of these things are our flowers. Children come from our flowers; kind and loving people in our lives come from the good deeds we sow, and our life's work comes from the things we create. The real beauty of the flower is not only in the blossom, it is in all the things that come because of us—even after we are gone.

Remember from Day 6: Mikiztli represents the skull and it has flowers on it; those flowers represent how we still blossom, how our ideas, accomplishments, children and anything we have created continue to blossom even after we have gone. These all keep creating and blossoming forever.

One of the most beautiful things we see are the flowers. Their beauty inspires us. We must put all of our love, effort and heart into the things we create. If we don't, we will not fully achieve our destiny. To make beautiful flowers we must find that joy and happiness in our lives, and when we really apply ourselves we can enjoy the things we have made and achieve our ultimate destiny. Remember the flowers are something we give to others; this is how they see us. This is an expression of our essence. In this way we transcend our lives; we are living in these flowers.

What others do with the flowers we give them is their choice. But we are still living in the things we create as long as we made them with all of our spirit and love.

Exercises

• Are you growing flowers? What are they?

• Do you think of yourself as a beautiful flower? Describe it.

• Now it is time to create and recognize beautiful flowers. This is the challenge; are you ready?

Worksheet

Worksheet

Worksheet

Conclusion to Exercises

With what symbol do you feel the most connected? Which one do you feel the most disconnected from? Sometimes our best quality can be our biggest handicap, but we can turn it into its fullest potential. Work on the symbols that you are stuck with to motivate yourself to grow. You must also understand your strengths and weaknesses. Be humble instead of arrogant, and share what you know. And, be willing to learn from others.

Make a list of the way that you relate to the symbols by numbering them 1-20, number 1 being the one you relate to the most, and 20 the least. Give your reasons why.

Worksheet

Worksheet

Worksheet

What's Next?

Now we have begun to know the twenty-day symbols. We must remember that everything we have read is now in the past. If we read it again, it will already have changed; we are not the same, and are constantly changing. This is the physical and spiritual life. Go through the book again and see if you still like your responses. Add to them or change them. You may not like any of your answers, but this only means that you are in motion. You are not stagnating or sitting back, but instead are coming into balance. This message is not about making you similar to others, it is about you being whatever you are—completely!

The human experience gives us the ability to think uniquely, to be whatever we are supposed to be. Every one of us has similarities, yet we are each unique. We must find balance in our own lives, then we find ourselves happier and healthier working in the communities we belong to.

Nothing in this book is a secret, nor are these new ideas. These day symbols were chosen for a reason, and they were carved in stone for us to be able to use. They are the flowers and songs of the Ancestors. They left us a message, and now we all can understand that message better.

Now, it's time to grow our flowers and make our songs. Each of the symbols also has many aspects in the way they were carved. Circles, dots and shapes all have something to do with aspects of the universe. We are part of the universe. This means we are also part of creation. We are not separate, above or below creation, we are a part of it. We are able to create, and we are changing along with creation.

Our struggles in life come when we fight against the changes that occur naturally. Never forget that everything is in motion. We can be responsible for the changes in our lives, and we can direct them through our actions. We can create a totally new outlook and start to live differently at any given moment. We can influence those around us, but we cannot change them. Change comes on a personal level. Yes it is true, there is strength in a group working toward common goals and being with people who share our views; however each one of us is unique and at the same time, part of the "all".

We can make dramatic change overnight but we can also take our time, evaluate and begin with the one thing that starts us in the direction we need to go. We must begin somewhere, and the start is the hardest part. Once started movement and motion are easier to maintain. Sometimes it takes a group of people to start to move the rock but only one to keep it in motion!

We hope with the help of this book, we are able to see where we are in our lives, and what we need to do to become the beautiful flowers that we are.

Now together, we are walking a new path. This road will take us to find our real face which is our essence. We will walk together sharing moments. These moments may sometimes be difficult, sad, bitter, or happy. Sometimes we walk with many on the same path and sometimes we are walking by ourselves. But we understand and accept that this walk follows the rhythm to the natural cycles of the universe.

When we realize these cycles and the rhythms of the cycles, it is like we are dancing. And dancing in the Toltec culture is the beautiful expression of walking and living in the best way. Follow the beat and create with the beat of the universe.

We become the ultimate expression. We become flowers because we feel the profound meaning to our existence, to our Tonalli, and our Tonalli inspires us. These emotions become thoughts, and those thoughts we bring into our actions; and those actions become an expression in words, and those words become our songs.

We started with an invitation to join in the challenge, and that challenge was the beginning of our willingness to live, to enjoy, and to feel happiness. So each instance and each breath, whether it is a great thing or the smallest thing, will be precious.

When we find ourselves, we will find our Tonalli, and then realize we are the flowers, and we are the songs.

Thank you for spending your time with our book. We all have a destiny but we must also learn to love the journey, and to understand our own personal and unique journey. Only you are able to do that for yourself. Now let the journey begin!

The Hidden Messages

En la casa de la niebla Mixkalli,
florecen cantos, se hacen cantantes,
se tejen petates de muchos colores.
Los libros se crean a si mismos,
Hablan y son escuchados…
Ojala no se marchiten,
Ojala no sean olvidados.

In the house of the Mist, Mixkalli,
songs flourish, everything becomes singers,
mats are wove from many colors,
The books create themselves,
they talk and they are being listened to.
I hope they don't wither,
I hope they are not forgotten.

La flor amarilla de ocho petalos,
tiene el aroma de luna y agua.
Verde es el mono con sombra roja,
Flor y mono elevan sus cantos,
13 y 19 veces, hasta que su voz…
Se torna blanca luz.

The yellow flower of eight petals,
Has the aroma of the moon and the water.
Green is the monkey with his red shadow,
flower and monkey lift their songs
13 and 20 times until their voices...
Turn in to white light.

Negro es el pensar, rojo el recordar;
Amarillo percibir, blanco es saber;
Verde es el vivir y azul es felicidad.
El hombre un ramo de flores
Con todos los colores y todos los aromas.

Black is the thought, red is remembering,
Yellow is to perceive, white is the knowledge.
Green is to live and blue is happiness.
The human is a bouquet of flowers,
With all the colors and all the aromas.

OME TEOTL

In Mexikayotl Yeliztli aik Ixpolihuiz.

Naui Ollin

INFO ABOUT SEMINARS
in the US and retreats in Mexico

website: www.asimpletruth.org

email: asimpletruth20@gmail.com